Are You Casablanca

by John Siwicki

ISBN 0-9792622-0-8
ISBN13 978-0-9792622-0-3

For Library of Congress Cataloging-in-Publication Data
please contact publisher

Poetic Art Published by:

SLABYPRESS
W25952 State Road 95
Arcadia, WI 54612
U.S.A.

CHEERS

Technical, Cover, and Book design by JBS

For information contact:
slabypress@yahoo.com

-Poems-

Tritoma

A Basket of Flowers

A world full of flowers
carried by my friend
Weaved together
so beautiful to see

Looking for a place to rest
next to a stream
On a hill or under a tree
Soft grass between my toes
Brushing tall flowers
with my fingertips

Upward to the sky
Sunshine falls on my face
All free nothing to buy
Could be the perfect place

Viburnum

I hear—I see water splashing
over the rocks
It reminds me of a bride
with a veil over her face

Steps of stones
go up along the hill
Stopping for a moment
Standing still, clouds float by
flags of the world
they wave high

Bees and butterflies
fly between the trees
Heart pounds every breath
Lone plum tree in the path
Beads of glistening juice
falling to the grass

Rolling down the hill
Drinking spring water
bubbling out of the ground
and laughing drunk

Watsonia

Scent of hot air
tickles my nose
Crystal leaves flicker—shake
—drop to the ground

Fields of flowers wide
Bright rainbow above a hill
Only one basket I have to fill
Into the basket the flowers go
for a gift, a present—
thanks and love

No strings attached
Give nothing in return
A basket of flowers
For love that burns
For love that's whole
Feeding the fire in my soul

~JS

Yarrow

Come Inside

Come inside to me
I'll give you a place to hide
Come inside to me
I'll protect you I cried
By the hand hold on tight
Follow me through the night
Careful, don't slip or fall
Listen, the wind will call
One more word to you
Then silent we become
Run fast at my side
Never let go of the bond
Your soft touch
Forever and beyond
Nothing ever I've loved so much
An embrace we are free
Open sky above
A blanket of stars open and wide
Come inside to me
I'll protect you I cried

~JS

Liatris

Three Lights on a Post

Cars race down the street
Footsteps on the pavement
Raindrops bouncing
out of puddles of water
Reflections of street lights
brilliant and bright
Wind blowing in the night
A girl I've never seen
soaked to the bone
standing under a tree
Then she looks at me
Lights on her face roll up
into the halo lit sky
Raindrops let go of her hair
and pass down
into the invisible ground
like a ghost
Above her there's a glow
Three lights on a post
There they shine
Sounds turn my head

Lisianthus

Shadows echo in the silky street
My eye follows until they melt
into the darkness
Now no one
sits under the lamp post
Just an empty bench
waiting for a passenger
to guide through the night
I taste mist in the air
Morning will come soon
Night disappears into the moon
Three lights pierce the night
The rain has stopped
and the mist is gone
A figure walks into my sight
over to the bench
to rest for the night
Another passenger for this
Indiscriminate host
The new passenger gazes around
Content with what he's found
Sanctuary for a little while
Night watches from all around

cidium

No light from the post
Morning noise and blue skies
People laugh, babies cry
Dogs bark, bicycles squeak
An empty bench
Servant for the tired and weak
The day over and sun down low
The three lights begin to glow
And then a girl I've never seen
with lights on her face
looks at me
Is she there on the bench
or only a dream?
A reflection from the street
passenger for the night
waiting for someone
Three lights, one shadow
go before the day comes
A voice in my mind whispers
I carefully step from the curb
and slowly cross the street
into a world of reflection
of day and night

~JS

Phalaenopsis Spray

Wife

Love is what I feel
Friendship
Is what we have
A hug, a kiss, a smile
When I think of you
Happy thoughts
Come my way!

~JS

Alstroemeria

Not Fantasy

Flying high above the trees

Is the music of life

It can be seen

As well as heard

Tasted, felt, and eaten

Every sense

Caresses our body

Our soul

This is real

On the table

Grasp it before it's gone

Life is not fantasy

It's a dream!

~JS

aryllis

For All

cry-smile-scream

live-love-dream

sit-stand-stare

hope-wish-dare

touch-taste-feel

remember-think-speak

youth-age-time

see-witness-show

care-help-share

recollect-know-forget

idea-imagine-create

gift-grace-salvation

~JS

Banksia

Chemical

Sweet mixture, taste, smell
What is it, I can't tell

Carried by people
Passed through the air
Floating wildly without a care

Then it hits, a knockout punch
Down for the count
Dazed a bit, but wanting more

Invisible and not for sale . . .

How is it acquired?
Who makes it?
Is it different for everyone?

Special formulas that match
Each individual person perfectly

Puzzles with pieces
That can't be seen . . .

Am I carrying a chemical?

Bouvardia

Is someone waiting for it now?
I wonder who?
How will I know?
When it's passed on

This craving never disappears
It lingers continuously
Keeping one aware and alert

When this euphoric time
Transpires . . .
I enter a endless circle
Spiraling into an unfurled run

The answer to this cryptic mystery
Veiled to all . . .
Until contact with an equal
To harmonize . . .

Then just as it splashes upon one
This falling, floating bubble
Vanishes into unseen space
Along with the radiant chemical

Releases the mighty grip
Frees itself . . .
Cascades on to another
Lodestone breath

~JS

Daffodil

Billetdoux

Standing there for the first time
Beauty, youth, eyes that care
Vibrant emotion, heart-beat climb
Fire on the wind, together soaring
Above mountains, higher than clouds
Out and away from the crowds
Sweeping the shore to the sea
Unforgettable memories stay
Smile, expression of joy
Word, song, special melody
Hands of love gently caress
Resting on pillows, soft as clouds
My arm covers my brow
Grasp one last brilliant moment
Hope that image will come true
But this is just the dream of a boy

~JS

Delphinium

Bond of Love

Bond of love - Unbroken chain
Never apart - Will always remain

Bond of love - Memory to keep
In my thoughts - At night I sleep

Bond of love - Today and beyond
A wish come true - Coin tossed in a pond

Bond of love - Meant to be free
Mind and soul - Two hearts agree

Bond of love - In my arm
Together and close - Safe from harm

Bond of love - Your hand in mine
This warm touch - Under stars that shine

Bond of love – Footsteps on the ground
A trail of our life – Love is found

~JS

Eremurus

BlinK

In the blink of an eye
The tear that falls
Has a love that holds on tight
In the blink of an eye
The smile I see
Has joy that fills an empty heart
In the blink of an eye
The hardest thing I ever said
Was goodbye
No matter how far or how long
We are apart
We stand together
You're forever in my heart

~JS

Freesia

Saint Remy

A wall that surrounds
Exhausted come to rest
But there is no rest
Only a schedule to keep
Love breaks free from life
Becomes unrelenting passion
Day—night . . . twists . . . turns
Visions suspended in air
Change seen by all
To an image in mind
Slice of a moment in time
. . . Painted on canvas
. . . Hung on a wall
Colors flowing in a frame . . .

~JS

Genistra

Inertia

Throughout our body it flows
Pressure, gravity and hope
Forward, up, around—down
Small universal living body
Following light, losing night
Traveling long distance—far
Returning again, changing site
Perpetual, liberating adventure
Energy, mass, total control
In concert, keeping time
Asleep, awake, stop and roll
Heartbeat, pumping love . . .
A living, growing vine . . .
Weight of the dimensional world
Floating through a narrow window
Threads of life . . . cosmic love

~JS

Weather

Love to Touch

Skin soft to touch
Skin of color and size
Breathing-growing-changing
delicate as a flower
Tough oak-age by sight
bending in the wind
soaking up the light
drinking water to live-taking root
Leaving home-scars of life
Making me strong-friends-neighbors
Blood kin-memories all wait within
Floating away-returning
again-looking different-a change
Feels the same-touch of love
Wife-children-mother-sister-brother
People I know-I say hello to the dog
in the street-fur soft-bird's wing
The breeze-silk-fine-glass of wine
Caress the face-touch the lace
Leaves that glow-flowers bloom
Spring-my wedding ring-musical
instrument that sings-wood-wire
Brass-leather stretched over a barrel

Hyacinth

Echoes of sound touch me
Passing through an invisible spirit
honest and true-cold heat too
Extreme-waking up after a kiss
Was it a dream-birthday present
next to my bed-joyful child-big
oak tree with roots above ground
A place a free mind can see
Climb to the top-hide between
Round and round seasons change the
ground under my feet-in my toes
fall on my nose-sunshine above
Things I love-touch-face-hand
A book with words to tell me
how a person looks-falling as
raindrops bounce up to the sky
Sand in the desert-hot and dry
Wise man met the mountain top
scrambling there to be alone
Now wise mountain climbed
the journey comes to an end.
Alone myself-love I leave
Life we weave will touch-
everyone we meet

~JS

Blanca Lily

Are you Casablanca

With fragrance
She stole my soul

With beauty
She captured my heart

Enchanted glances
Embrace across the room

Dance of love
Spinning, dizzy, falling

Senses wake
I hesitate

Fleeting moments I hold
But may never come again

Priceless memory
A wish to touch yesterday

Secret love—absolute
Precious and until—love always

~JS

IXIA

A Feeling

My breath taken away
By a soft gentle heart

Love given to me
Held open and free

Felt in time
Always never ending

~JS

Larkspur

Moment of Love

Young she stands
There with a friend
Talking and laughing

Is she alone?
I wonder?

She looks at me
Now I know
Just from a glance

Over to her I go
Hello I say

A moment of torture
A moment of sweetness
A moment of love

~JS

Kangaroo Paw

Love Struck

Not so often does it happen
A feeling that takes me away

It's special and rare
An explosion through air

There's no way to control
What turns out of hand

Over and under to the end
Tangled mind, the front behind

The color of wild love
Thunder—lightning from above

~JS

Leptospermum

Waiting Forever

Does it come soon
Time, another day
After a while it goes

Facing one direction
Turn to the right
Again, again, again

Sit on the ground
Tired, then lie down
Roll over, stop

I close my eyes
I fall asleep
A voice flies

The dream has begun
I wake, now it's over
Here I wait again

~JS

Protea

Amore

Clever girl she is that's sure
FInding answers to riddles

A hearty laugh sings with joy
Soft gentle eyes that shine

Friendly greeting warmly given
Saying hello and goodbye

With her I can be myself
This I know and feel

But never a moment alone
Like time—changed—grown

~JS

Queen Annee Lace

Some Days

Women I love
The reason why
How it happens

Sharp wit, a smile
A gentle ringing voice
Gestures of affection

More I want to know
Try to understand
A long difficult task

A smile of joy
Read on her face
Long lasting image

Then the time for goodbye
A search for what to say
Why does it have to be . . .

. . . this way

~JS

Red Ginger

Magic

There-I was there-in the right place
Electricity surged, charged, pulsated
A million thoughts ran through me

I looked-my feet-still on the ground
A fragrance floated into my mind
No doubt what was happening

Sound rang-a sweet melody
Rhythm carried on gentle voice
Breath lost without mind

The door opened-I walked through
My hand outstretched to touch
Soft pattern, a parallel line

From a distance-voices spoke
Time still ticked, but did not exist
Emotion on the quay, ready to burst

Together-finally the release
Until another day, another beginning
The rhythm, the melody, the voice

Always remembered-special time
On that day, always, but never again
A memory never forgotten

~JS

Rattlesnake Calathium

Another Dance

Music floating through the air
One step, then two, three
Notion, motion, emotion

A quick step and race
Leading, following, chasing
Latching on to the sound

Gentle, slow step to make
Caress softly, time to wake
I see her, look at her, hold her

Together, we touch, again
A moment on the dance floor
Lost in time no more

Found, the love of my life
The fountain that flows
A dream that forever grows . . .

~JS

Snapdragon

Augar

Not with a crystal ball or palm
Not with cards spread on a table
Not with tea leaves in water

Not read from the stars above
Not told in stories from a dream
Where everything passes soon

But in her eyes
The moment of truth
Bright as a midnight moon

That's where I saw love

~JS

Star Gazer Lily

Love on a Bicycle

A wheel for me
One for you
Two wheels three

Coasting, gliding, floating
Working hard on the grade
On the top, bottom, or side

Blood rushes in my veins
My skin turns vibrant red
I yell, moan, cry, cringe

Soft, gentle, calm desires
Hunger, thirst, out of breath
Exhausted, without power

That was fun
Meet tomorrow, again?
Will you come?

I feel—free—free—free . . .

~JS

Statice

Breakers

A wave breaking onto the shore
Tears rolling down my face

Angry voice, growling wildly
Destroying the fragile lace

Pushing further until powerless
Gone, nothing left, no clue or trace

There in sight on the horizon
With a beat and steady pace

This dance, turning and spinning
Speed and flight, balance and grace

A gamit of emotion we all live
This is common for the human race

What—where, does the secret lie
A treasure stored hidden encased

Never pulled from sacred ground
buried deep in an unknown place

~JS

Star of Bethlehem

Never see her again

I feel the weight of the world
My mind trapped with her vision
Her laugh a signal to my ear
What is on her mind?
Am I wrong to believe—love?

The thoughts of her burned
Embedded forever deep
Why am I silent today?
Yesterday the first day
Her words remembered

Wisdom what does it teach
To be careful, well behaved
An old mortal I've become
Time will not last . . .
Please show me a hint, a clue

Is it me that doesn't know?
That's the signal perhaps
But when she looks at me
Her glow takes over my soul
From her I'll never be free

~JS

Sunflower

Beauty in the Morning

Sound dances to my ear
Sweet, natural, so sincere
My eyes still closed tight

Gently the breeze touches me
Movement alive with energy
Raising me from my slumber

The day that is to come
Time to play and have fun
Power and strenth slowly return

What will happen is a surprise
Could be the truth or all lies
It always begins in the mind

~JS

phantasmagoria

All I hear is the rain pouring down
From the dark, cloudy sky
Similar to a machine's din
On a relentless journey downward
Slapping homeward against the windows
Not with complaint, but enjoyment
Being pummeled, drop after drop

Outside the leaves of the trees and plants
Are spanked by the drops of falling liquid
Gradually the relentless torrent
Sounds different from rain-
An angry thunder, a tempest, a lion's roar
Fierce, angry, savage...

Then the volume transforms itself
As I listen to it collide into the roof
A hammer driving a path
Desiring to go down

Flat on my back, safe in my bed
I lie with my eyes and mind wide open
As my senses absorb the night

The ceiling begins to glow brightly
Twinkling stars from another galaxy
So close yet possible to grasp
Up to the boundless frontier my hands go
Desiring to hold the stars with my fingertips

Slowly dancing through the air
Until they freely surrender
Unable to break free from my arms
Acting as a leash handcuffing my hands
Clutching them close to my body

My digits begin to move independently
Putting on a show, bending back and forth
With this galaxy of stars as a backdrop...

Shapes sprout from the vast world I see
Suddenly they burst forth, alive and graceful
As I view this display, I plunge into a feeling
Of expectation and notions...

Energy from the storm alive in my mind
Thunder, lightning, a tornado...
Spinning through my imagination...
With me as the guide---

Just then in the confusion of the storm
Eyes close, I melt into a dream world
Perhaps I'll remember this night

My heartbeat rocks me into a trance
Eyelids fluttering kinship to the raindrops
As I hear the beads rap and roll
Down the window into an infinite cosmos

I hear violins singing to each other
As I fall through puffy white clouds
My body glistening from rays of sunshine
Reflecting off of my body
The violins change into chirping birds
Hunting for their breakfast

I feel now is my time!
Walls to tear down, chains to break
Fences to cross, one more step
No fear dancing with the stars
Every day I have breath...

I recall being quizzed at an early age
About why I could not sit still
I had no patience or forbearance
But at times captivated for hours

Building objects from wood and plastic
Able to focus as the sun beats down
Relentlessly melting everything in its view
Oblivious to everything and everyone

Feeling the sense to get away
Moving across time in silence...

Going fast, the experience a blur
Almost a dream-like memory
Watching my feet stir
In a slow-motion fashion

Counting the steps I'd taken
Measuring the distance and the time
Observe progress, watching change

Flawless melodies
Singing snapshots of life

Now my journey begins nevertheless
Without any plan or thought
Changing direction sharply on the spur
Striking familiarity, caused by chance
Not knowing the destination

Is a breath of fresh air
All I know is the turning of the earth
Round and round, night and day

Joy - love - desire - passion - comfort – peace

So near yet so distant...

Separated and isolated from me
A pagination of unfolding fences
Fences that harbor vast areas
Where only few are allowed

Harsh, mournful fences that slowly
Crumble and wither with time
Leaving only a blemish, a scar of the past

A lifetime is sometimes needed
To breach the mangled walls of iron

First view horrifies, then shocks the sweet
Seen as protection at first, then barrier
Shielding the powerful from the languid
As roads are traveled, reason is lost...
A new dream takes its place

Invisible fences are now
Blocking progress and change
Perhaps only realized for a moment

Tide coming in and going out
Without a visible bridge
No door, gateway or opening
Struggle for life...
Every second-minute-hour-day-
Year after year...

The fence of time and space
Controls our existence...

A fence made long ago...
This novelty greeted with open arms
Enriching life... weaving a fabric of labor

Eventually my weary mind weakens
Tired from the relentless ticking of time

The fence of time
Has proved to be too mighty
Shall I rest for a few moments?
Fear of not waking spurs me on

All alone in the desert
Walking along the highway
Looking for something
On the other side of the horizon
Where I am is an empty place

No sound, only wind and my footsteps
Withering like an old piece of wood
Soon the mountains are in distant sight
Fences of stone...
That appear impossible to climb!

Clouds in the sky change into faces
My father is one that I recognize

He urges me to follow and go on
The faces move across the sky on the wind

I enter a massive mountain range...

Emphatic, determined, powerful
Triumphant, I rejoice...
At the summit, I'm liberated
I rejoice in victory!
There the stars are again looking down

An outstretched arm, a fingertip away
Imagining what is behind or beyond...

Off I go to the other side...
Washed by the glowing gleam
I fall off into my dream

Gazing in silence up at raindrops of light
Humming songs to keep the pain
Of my journey away

Tall pines that reach to the sky
Close in around me

The steps taken earlier
Now beat along with my heart

Sounds of the night pierce my mind
I cover my eyes

My face and breath feel warm
No longer tired or weary
My muscles stretch and retract
With power and energy
After deep breaths of fresh, cool, sweet air

I'm off to climb the next fence that waits
Soon the weight of my tired eyes
Proves too powerful, I drift and doze…
Memories spring out of my mind!

Flying in a plane filled with soldiers going home
Bright sun, cold crisp air, hard as stone
Tender loving smiles, safe and secure
A rumbling roar, sharp, rough and raw
Slicing from above and beneath
Thunder passing, learning the law…

Holding our breath, falling safely down
Soon we're all safe on the ground
After crossing a perpetual welkin

On a tricycle, the curly-head boy smiles
With melted ice cream on his face
This all on a bright summer day

Fences that block our way are clear
Some made by others to turn us away
Or fences to gaze upon for years
We build them until they are done
Kind words, love's soft touch, and help
From this, no fence will stand

No chain will hold
The energy of the storm will unfold
All things are but a moment away...

One old, three-story brick house
A good-sized yard, a garden filled
Growing flowers, vegetables, happiness
Bordering a tree line
Near a small parcel of woods
Leading down to a small stream
Where children are wading and playing

See the old screen door of the house
My hand reaches out, the door opens
An old rusty spring squeaks as it stretches

I enter a large hallway with many rooms
Old wooden trim...
Wraps windows and doorways

Up the stairway, round and round...
Up to the third floor
Solid, warm, beautiful oak under my feet
A box kite leaning against the wall
Ready for flight, but where's Grandpa?
I want to fly his kite

Stepping over to the window, glance outside
He is in the garden planting seeds and flowers
A dog barks and runs through the backyard
Chasing boys of a childhood language
Carefully through the garden
Into the woods and down the hill
Across the creek
I cannot see but know what's there...

The children have no problem
Crossing this fence of shallow water
Along the bank, the three-mile waterfall
The rusty, ancient, obsolete bridge
Paint peeling and falling to the ground
Blowing away in the wind
Shaking and rattling while being crossed

A good diving point
Into the pond below the falls
But they prove too great
For the young to ford
Fear, not wisdom, tells them to wait
But this will be the last time
For courage is needed to decide one's fate

Many roads are taken, fences are crossed
Rush to judgement, a careless fall
Lessons learned and never forgotten
My old home with the squeaky door
School playground
Big, oak tree across the street

Old three-story house
Filled with a lifetime of memories
Memories, stacks of photos packed away
In the closets are albums
Filled with a world of flavors
Waiting to be opened, taking the curious
Off to a dream world fantasy of life
Places and astounding drama
Angles and timeless images

I am part of this fantasy
Stored away, waiting for the next witness
Called to survey and discover
This extraordinary place of impression
I've seen people grow old
But through the pictures...
I see them, as they were long ago

A delineation of boys and girls
Women and men, brothers and sisters
They all live in this panorama of memories
Available to anyone who opens the door

Sentimental feelings bubble to the surface
I recollect the images frozen in time
Unrecognizable children at first
My sisters and brothers I soon know

Myself, a small child standing in the kitchen
Hands in my pockets and shoes untied
Not knowing how to pose for the camera

Watching my sister dance
To a melody I can't hear
Pictures of people I've never met

European towns and cities
That have long since changed
A journey to my parents' wedding
Being born allows me to see
Where it took place, what they wore

It reminds me of a scene
From an old black and white movie
Classic with character
A world since forgotten

The military father wore his uniform
Full dress, sharp with badges
Medals and rank

Placing a golden ring
On my mother's hand
Making a promise
Taking a vow this day

Standing with her hand in his
Grasp of love, heartfelt stare
Kiss on the lips...
She wore a dark, genteel suit
Spangled white dots tinged with ivory
Shone a starlit night of radiance
All this in one afternoon, one night
Wedding, dance, celebration...
Looking at picture albums
Locked in a trance

Some relatives, a few friends
Uncles and aunts
People I don't recall

Children that will grow
Soldiers new found love
Blue sky above...

Land that is part of me
Country in my hand, my life
Under my fingernails, deep in my skin
In my blood, flowing through my soul

Celebration, candles on the cake
New bicycle, off to the path lined with trees
A hot summer day, a cool soft breeze

Fishing with dad, fishing with friends
Campfire under the stars, dancing fire light
Sounds of the night, water rolling on rocks

Footsteps that become silent
Content, no idea of the time...
Waiting for the next day to shine
Then smiling faces, this day is new

I see a field and my dad on a horse
Wholeness of man and beast, strong allies
Coupled in a marvelous partnership
Until one is no more...

Heads held high, ready to ride
Over the tall grass, they gallop in stride

A glance at me
Face of wisdom, hair of gray
Down to my hand with an iron grip
He pulls me over the saddle
My arms wrap around him tightly
I smell his life...

To the horizon we gallop
Floating on the breeze
Across the field, along the woods
Running fast...
Sliding off the saddle
Hanging on for my life
This makes me grip him more
He turns to me with a smile
"Now is the time to become as one!"

I see the fence grow near
Wide-open eyes gaze with fear
Fingertips tingle, muscles grow tense
Closer and closer, hooves of thunder
Listening to the horses pant, then silence...

Forever it felt to float above the fence
On that day, this I saw...

Clear the fence and earthbound law
There is a way, on my lips I prayed...

This fence we clear today!
With your help Lord, a strong horse we need!

Down to the ground we breeze...
As I turn behind, I see the fence still there
On the horse, father and son

For this day, we had no fear
Together again, one last fence to clear
Then off into the sunset, we disappear...

millie's trip

Over and over she asked, "When can we go?
I'm ready! What are we waiting for? Lets go!"
So today is the day, pump up the tires
Oil the chain and check the breaks

Out the gate we went and up the hill fast
To the first intersection
No fear, a very brave little girl
Then down the hill holding the breaks
Careful and calm she rode, amazed I stood
She had learned well, improved her skill
This was real bike riding
Not in the yard or in the park...

Alert she was as we approached a steep hill
What a hill! How would she do?
A first-time experience, this was all new
We stopped to take a look
Her confidence and courage shone through
Soon she would go on bike rides alone
Down the hill, rolling fast at high speed
She held the bike straight and true
Enjoying every moment until the last

And then we went into a store
What we bought is a forgotten thought
Only the bike ride, I remember that day
After some time we were on our way

"What about the hill on the way home?
It is very steep! Do we walk?" she asked
"This time the hill we climb," I said

On the bike she stood
Pushing with all of her might and heart
Around the peddles went slowly
"Peddle hard, peddle hard
We'll make it to the top, push hard!"

Once there, we took a drink and felt the joy
This special moment, once in a lifetime
For the rest of the trip, I then knew
Millie's first step and now a bike ride too
The world, an adventure she'll go and seek
This first bike ride is our memory to keep
When we talk of that day
Pride and joy I feel
My little girl has grown fast and high
Special and precious days have passed

born in austria

Morning rises, night sets
Just like any other place

Flags blow in the wind
Tablecloths of lace

Old wood, tall mountains
Fresh air to breathe

Sweet music plays
Pastry tickles the tongue

Mine and Mozart's home
Many songs are sung

Stay for a time
Make new friends

A birthplace found
To someday return

On my face this is worn
Austria is where I was born

<u>for all</u>

cry-smile-scream...

live-love-dream...

sit-stand-stare...

hope-wish-dare...

touch-taste-feel...

remember-think-speak...

youth-age-time...

see-witness-show...

care-help-share...

recollect-know-forget...

idea-imagine-create...

gift-grace-salvation...

natural

Rocks, grass, earth...
      -roots down deep-
Sweat, water, ice...
      -rain on my face-
Birds, butterflies, rabbits...
      -path in the trees-
Sky, clouds, stars...
      -dream in my mind-
Thunder, lightening, fire...
      -wild-burning energy-
Tears, joy, laughter...
      -emotions from the heart-
Running, jumping, falling...
      -actions experienced everyday-
Handshake, hug, kiss...
      -hello, I miss you-
Walking, eating, sleeping...
      -becomes a daily routine-
Party, dance, life...
      -the best time I've ever had-
Time, forever, eternity...
      -a day in the sun-

Poetry

Inflexation
Fences
The Poetry of Food and Drink
Warblings

Novels

ExPRESSION
AWAKE ASLEEP DREAMING DEAD